The Wild Outdoors

GO PADDLEBOARDING!

by
Heather E. Schwartz

Published by Capstone Press, an imprint of Capstone
1710 Roe Crest Drive, North Mankato, Minnesota 56003
capstonepub.com

Library of Congress Cataloging-in-Publication Data
Names: Schwartz, Heather E., author.
Title: Go paddleboarding! / Heather E. Schwartz.
Description: North Mankato, Minnesota : Capstone Press, [2023] | Series:
The wild outdoors | Includes bibliographical references. | Audience:
Ages 8–11 | Audience: Grades 4–6 | Summary: Enjoy calm waters and a
warm, sunny day on a paddleboard! Readers will learn about the skills
and equipment they need to go paddleboarding. Find out important
safety rules and ways to protect the environment, all while having fun
experiencing this outdoor activity!—Provided by publisher.
Identifiers: LCCN 2021057065 (print) | LCCN 2021057066 (ebook) | ISBN
9781666345773 (hardcover) | ISBN 9781666345780 (paperback) | ISBN
9781666345797 (pdf) | ISBN 9781666345827 (kindle edition)
Subjects: LCSH: Stand-up paddle surfing—Juvenile literature.
Classification: LCC GV840.S68 S35 2023 (print) | LCC GV840.S68 (ebook)
|DDC 798.5—dc23/eng/20211223
LC record available at https://lccn.loc.gov/2021057065
LC ebook record available at https://lccn.loc.gov/2021057066

Image Credits

Alamy: North Wind Picture Archives, 7; Getty Images: Cavan Images, 19,
DE AGOSTINI PICTURE LIBRARY, 6, Krista Long, 17, praetorianphoto,
1, 13, SolStock, 24, waterotter, 21; Newscom: mavrixphoto, 9; Shutterstock:
Erickson Stock, 5, 23, EvgeniiAnd, Cover, homydesign, 11, Irina Wilhauk,
20, Iryna Kalamurza, 27, Lilkin, 14, lunamarina, 29, Marzolino, 8, Natalia
Duryagina, 16, rdonar, 15, Sanchik, 26, StockFamily, 25

Editorial Credits

Editor: Erika L. Shores; Designer: Dina Her; Media Researchers:
Jo Miller and Pam Mitsakos; Production Specialist: Tori Abraham

All internet sites appearing in back matter were available and accurate
when this book was sent to press.

Table of Contents

Words in **bold** are in the glossary.

JUST FOR FUN

Even if you've never been out paddleboarding, this outdoor activity looks fun to try. It's easy to imagine paddling along quietly on the water. Standing on a long, flat board, you're in command of your destiny. You can paddle wherever you want to go.

In reality, paddleboarding may not be as easy as it looks, especially in the beginning. It takes some practice to balance on the board. You'll also need to learn to steer, so you can control the direction of the board. After you have the basics down, you'll find out paddleboarding is a great way to experience nature. This activity lets you explore while enjoying yourself on the water.

FACT

All ages enjoy paddleboarding. In 2020, about 3.7 million people took part in the activity in the United States.

People use a long paddle to row a paddleboard.

Chapter 1

WHERE IT ALL BEGAN

The history of paddleboarding dates back thousands of years. But long ago, it wasn't thought of as an activity to do for fun and adventure. It was simply a method of getting around in the water. Like paddleboarding today, it involved standing up on a watercraft and using a paddle to move.

An engraving from the 1800s shows people using a raft and poles on the water.

Standing up in a canoe allowed people to see into the distance better as they quickly paddled.

There's evidence that people all around the ancient world navigated the water this way. In Peru, fishermen created a watercraft out of reeds. They used a long piece of bamboo in place of a modern paddle. African warriors stood up in canoes that were hollowed out. They paddled with their spears. Indigenous people in North America also used canoes in this way.

A man standing to row a fishing raft

Modern paddleboarding got its start in Hawaii. Many people living in Hawaii have **Polynesian heritage**. Polynesians were among the ancient paddleboarders.

In the mid-1900s, some Hawaiian surf instructors started standing on their boards and using a paddle to get around while teaching students. Standing up, the instructors could see the waves better. They could also carry cameras and get great photos that tourists could take home with them. These photos were in high demand.

The idea of standing up on a surfboard with a paddle wasn't seen as a new outdoor activity right away. It finally took off in the early 2000s.

Pro surfer Laird Hamilton needed a way to train when the surf was down. He started paddleboarding. He got people excited when he used a paddle with a large American flag attached.

Laird Hamilton rowing a surfboard in 2008

Around the same time, pro surfer Rick Thomas traveled to Hawaii and saw paddleboarding in action. When he returned home to California, he had a custom paddle made to use with his surfboard. People loved seeing him demonstrate the activity.

Chapter 2

AWESOME ACTIVITY

Do you already enjoy canoeing or kayaking? Paddleboarding is one more way you can get out on the water. It could become your favorite water activity if you find you're more comfortable standing than sitting. You might discover the paddleboard is easier to steer than other watercraft.

If you like hiking or camping, you can bring a paddleboard along. That will motivate you to look for spots near lakes, rivers, or the ocean. You could find some new locations you've never visited before.

**Most people paddleboard in summer months because
the water temperature is warmer then.**

Unlike surfing, you don't need waves to
paddleboard. In fact, it's much better to start in
calm water. And while it's easy to imagine getting
out during the summer, warm weather isn't required
either. Paddleboarding is a sport you can do even in
the cooler months. You'll just need to wear a wetsuit
or other waterproof clothing.

While you're learning to paddleboard, you'll build strength. It takes muscle to balance, paddle, and steer. This full-body workout has other health benefits too. When you're paddleboarding, you connect with nature. You need to focus on your environment. You likely don't have time to think about school problems or other stress. Taking a break from those worries is good for your mental health.

Some people **meditate** on a paddleboard. They stop paddling to sit on the board and move into different positions to relax their minds. Repetitive paddling can get you into a meditative state too. It is a calming activity.

As you learn to paddleboard, you're building confidence. Each time you go out, you have more control over the paddleboard. You decide where and how fast you want to go.

FACT

The largest paddleboard parade took place in Russia in 2017. It included 844 paddleboards.

**Rowing your paddleboard makes
your arm muscles stronger.**

Chapter 3

GETTING STARTED

Of course, you'll need a paddleboard and a paddle to get started with this outdoor activity. Inflatable paddleboards are easier to pack than hard boards. You can use a special air pump to inflate these boards once you reach your chosen location.

Pumping air into an inflatable paddleboard

Paddleboards come in different styles for recreational use, racing, and other activities. An all-around paddleboard is stable and good for beginners. Surf paddleboards are shorter and wider than other paddleboards. They perform better in waves.

Paddles come in different styles. Large blades are powerful, but you have to be stronger to use them. Some paddles are made of wood, which needs extra care so it won't rot. Others are made of carbon fiber, which is light and easy to use.

Board Basics

The top of the board is called the deck. The deck pad is the foam or rubber area where the paddleboarder stands. The nose is at the front end and the tail is at the back.

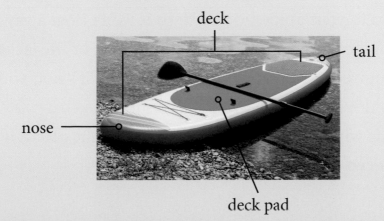

deck

tail

nose

deck pad

It's important to wear a paddleboard leash in choppy water so that you and your board don't get separated.

There are a few more items you'll need for a paddling adventure. A paddleboard leash attaches the board to your ankle by a cord, so it won't float away if you fall off. A personal floatation device, or life jacket, is required by law in most places. Even if it's not, you should wear one to stay safe. You must also carry a rescue whistle. That way you can sound the alarm if you need help.

As for clothing, a bathing suit or board shorts make the most sense. Use water-resistant sunscreen and reapply every two hours. Wear a rash guard for extra protection against the sun. These shirts are made to get wet and keep your skin safe from sunburn. Water shoes and a sun hat are good ideas too.

A long-sleeve rash guard keeps your arms, shoulders, and back from getting sunburned.

Getting on the board takes some skill. Start in knee-deep water close to the shore. Kneel on the center of the board. Then, step onto your feet one at a time to move to a standing position. To balance on the board, point your toes forward, so your feet are in a **parallel** position. Shift your weight at your hips as the water moves. Keep your eyes on the **horizon**—not your feet. This will make it easier to stay balanced.

Using the paddle requires learning the skills to move forward and backward and to turn. Each movement requires different **strokes**, or a combination of strokes. You also need to learn how to hold the paddle. Proper hand positioning will make it easier to move where you want to go. The handle at the top of the paddle is called the T-grip. It is attached to the blade by a long stick called a shaft. The front end of the blade is the tip.

Expert Help

The best way to learn how to paddleboard is to get out there and try it. You could also take lessons to learn the skills and gain confidence. A paddleboarding instructor can teach you everything you need to know, while helping you improve.

Use the T-grip to hold the paddle at the top. Hold
the shaft of the paddle with your other hand.

Chapter 4

SAFETY MATTERS

First time out? Still learning? Try a calm lake without a lot of boats making waves in the water. Look for a sandy beach where you can easily wade in from the shore. Paddleboarding in the ocean is doable. But in the beginning, it makes more sense to play it safer. You can work your way up to the challenges of ocean paddleboarding.

A calm spot without motorized boats and little wind is good for a first-time paddleboarder.

**Use the weather forecast to dress appropriately.
Do not stay on the water if you see lightning.**

With safety in mind, watch the weather. Choose a day that's not too windy for your outing. Make sure there aren't any storms in the forecast. You definitely don't want to be on the water in a thunder and lightning storm.

If you plan to go out in water that's over your head, you should have basic swimming skills. With a life jacket on, it's easiest to swim while floating on your back.

Falling off and getting back on the paddleboard are two more skills you should have when you head out. If you can, try to fall away from the board. You want to avoid hitting it on your way down. Don't try to grab your board. But do hang on to your paddle, if possible.

Once you're in the water, move to the center of the paddleboard. Hang on to the carry handle. Pull yourself up so you can reach the rail on the opposite side. With one hand on the carry handle and the other on the opposite rail, kick your legs and pull yourself up back on the board.

FACT

Some people paddleboard with their dog. Canine companions should wear life jackets too.

Chapter 5

CARE FOR THE ENVIRONMENT

When paddleboarders head for the water, they often travel through beaches or grassy areas to get there. These places are home to birds, insects, and other creatures. Plenty of plants grow near the water too. Whether you're on foot, on a bike, or in a car, stay on established paths. That way you won't trample the environment or cause extra **erosion**. If you're walking, wear light shoes that won't dig into the ground.

By using paths, you protect the animals and plants living near your paddleboarding spot.

Trash covers a sandy beach on the island of Bali.

Unfortunately, wherever humans travel, you'll find litter. Bring a trash bag on your adventures, so you can carry out any garbage you find on the ground. Of course, you can use the same bag for your own trash.

Many people collect sand, rocks, and shells as keepsakes. However, they should stay put. They don't belong in your house or yard. They're needed in the environment where you found them.

FACT

Elafonissi Beach, in Greece, is famous for its pink sand. So many people took the sand, it began to look less pink. It is now illegal to take it.

Chapter 6

PADDLEBOARD LIKE A PRO

People who love paddleboarding combine it with all sorts of other activities. For an added physical challenge, many boarders enjoy stand-up paddleboard (SUP) yoga. Doing yoga poses on a paddleboard isn't easy. But it's a great workout while you experience nature.

Fishing off a paddleboard is fun too. You'll need an anchor for this activity, so you don't float away from your chosen spot. You might also want an umbrella to create some shade. And bring a cooler to hold your big catch!

Doing yoga on a paddleboard is a calming activity for some people.

Paddleboarders compete in a race in France.

If you like to compete, you can even race on a paddleboard. Races are held for every level from beginner to expert. There are paddleboards and paddles made especially for racing. If you choose to race, you'll need to train so you can go the distance. That's usually 6 miles (9.7 kilometers) for beginners.

Hang out with other paddleboarders, and you might hear terms like SUP, iSUP, quiver, and grom. What does it all mean? It helps to know, even if you're a beginner.

SUP—an acronym for stand-up paddleboarding, another name for the activity

iSUP—an acronym for inflatable stand-up paddleboard

grom—a young paddleboarder

quiver—a collection of paddleboards for different activities and conditions

Spend a lot of time paddleboarding, and you're bound to learn more **lingo**. As you improve your skills and talk about this sport, you'll look and sound like an expert. You might start to feel like one too!

A grom SUP in the ocean

GLOSSARY

erosion (e-ROH-zhuhn)—the process by which something is worn away

heritage (HER-uh-tij)—history and traditions handed down from the past

horizon (huh-RYE-zuhn)—the line where the earth or a body of water seems to meet the sky

lingo (LIN-goh)—the special language used for a particular activity or by a particular group of people

meditate (MED-i-tayt)—to relax the mind and body by a regular program of mental exercise

parallel (PA-ruh-lel)—the same distance apart along the whole length, without touching

Polynesian (pall-ee-NEE-zhun)—native to islands of Polynesia; Hawaii has Polynesian heritage

stroke (STROHK)—one of a series of repeated arm movements used to move through the water

READ MORE

Gottschall, Meghan. *Go Paddling!* Minneapolis: Bearport Publishing Company, 2022.

Lyon, Drew. *Surfing and Other Extreme Water Sports.* North Mankato, MN: Capstone Press, 2020.

Towell, Colin. *Survival!: A Step-by-Step Guide to Camping and Outdoor Skills.* New York: DK Publishing, 2019.

INTERNET SITES

Paddle Boarding for Beginners: SUP Tips and Gear
bearfoottheory.com/stand-up-paddle-boarding-tips/

A (True) Beginner's Guide to Stand Up Paddleboarding
oars.com/blog/stand-up-paddleboarding-tips-for-beginners/

INDEX

ABOUT THE AUTHOR

Heather E. Schwartz writes books for kids from her home in upstate New York. She loves writing because she loves learning new things, brainstorming creative ideas, and moving words around on a page. Some of her favorite outdoor activities include downhill skiing, hiking, canoeing, kayaking, and paddleboarding.